PIANO • VOCAL • GUITAR

BEE GEES ANTHOLOGY

ISBN 978-0-7935-0413-8

HAL•LEONARD® CORPORATION

7777 W. BLUEMOUND RD. P.O. BOX 13819 MILWAUKEE, WI 53213

Contents

ALIVE

Words and Music by BARRY GIBB
and MAURICE GIBB

C#m
F#
A
lit - tle bit fast - er
'cause you've got a lit - tle less time to go.
E
A
E
A
I ain't lost and I ain't search - ing,
E
A
but then you know me ver - y well.

E
B/D#
C#m
And I can't change the wind _ and make it blow the oth - er way.
And I can't change the world _ and make it go the oth - er way.
F#
A
E
I'm a fool _ and I can tell _ that I'm a
F#
B
F#
B
live ___ and that's all, ___ that I can get up just as fast as I fall. ___ And I can
F#
B
F#
B
walk and run but I'll nev-er crawl. ___ And in the end it does-n't mat-ter at all. I ___ don't

E A B A
know a - bout_ the peo - ple that I read__ a - bout_ in books. And the kings_
E A B A
__ and queens_ a - round_ my room_ with their quiet dir - ty looks._ I know_
E A B A
__ I should_ be go - ing some-where, I just can't ar - rive._ There's a
E A E
To Coda
rea - son for be - liev - ing that I've nev - er been_ a - live.__

A
E
A
E
I ain't lost and I ain't
A
E
search - ing,
but then you know me ver - y
A
D.S. al Coda
well.
CODA
B
A
nev - er been a - live. I know

E A/E B/D♯ A
I should be go-ing some-where, I just can't ar-rive. There's a
E A B7 A
rea-son for be-liev-ing that I've nev-er been a-live.
E A
A-live, a-
E
live.

BODYGUARD

Words and Music by BARRY GIBB,
MAURICE GIBB and ROBIN GIBB

Cmaj9
Bm7
D/E
Am7
G
Bm7
G
It hurts me when you cry
when you feel the love is
Bm7
Cmaj7
Cm
gone.
Don't give up on us when you got so much to be - lieve in.

G Em Am7 /D G
And so I beg you please stay yeah. Dan-ger in the night,
Bm7 G Bm7
a flame that nev-er dies in a
C D Em Bm7 C Am7
world of lone-ly fa-ces you need some-one to sur-vive, a love like yours should nev-er live a-
/D
lone.
1.
Cmaj9
Let me be your bo - dy-guard,
(I can be use-ful to you)

Bm7
Cmaj9
we can just get ex - ci - ted, stop be-fore we go too far.
Let me be your bo - dy-guard.
Bm7
E
(liv-ing in my pro-tec - tion) we can just get ig - ni - ted, lost in-side
Am7
Cm
G
it's on - ly you and me.
2.
Bm7
Em
I know the signs and I'm tell-ing you you're liv - ing on bor-rowed time, but a

Am7
/D
heart needs love like a flo - wer needs rain, like I'm mak-ing you mine.
Cmaj9
Bm7
Let me be your bo - dy-guard, we can just get ex - ci - ted,
(I can be use-ful to you)
Cmaj9
stop be-fore we go too far. (liv-ing in my pro - tec - tion)
Let me be your bo - dy-guard
Bm7
Am7
we can just get ig - ni - ted, what we had nev-er known all our lives, I pray

Cm G Bm7 C
— it's not too late, — I would die by your side my love I'm the life that you
Cm A C#m7 A
save. — (Instr.)
C#m7 D E F#m7 C#m7
In this world of pain and sor-row eve-ry wish is your com-mand, — a
Bm7 G D/E C#m7
heart like yours should nev-er live a - lone. — I used to dream of a spe-cial one and

F♯m7
now I feel it com-ing true,
but I
Bm7
could-n't let go, I'm a jea - lous guy
/E
what you're put-ting me through.
Dmaj7
)
Let me be your bo - dy - guard
(I can be use-ful to you)
C♯m7
we can just get ex - ci - ted,
E
stop be-fore we go too far,
Dmaj7
let me be your bo - dy-guard
(liv-ing in my pro - tec - tion)
C♯m7
we can just get ig - ni - ted,

VERSE 2:
There's things you shouldn't do
You lose your self-control
Should the eyes of a perfect stranger
Take you down to a new sensation
Just turn back to me
Don't wait till it's gone
Don't go where you don't belong
In a world of pain and sorrow
Every wish is your command
A heart like yours
Should always find a home.

BOOGIE CHILD

Words and Music by BARRY GIBB,
MAURICE GIBB and ROBIN GIBB

Moderately, with a funky beat

B7
A7
Boo-gie; I can't stand the way you do it, boo-gie child.
B7
A7
B7
Boo-gie; bad girl, don't put me through this.
Boo-gie; right to the lim -
A7
B7
A7
it, boo-gie child.
Boo-gie; you're a bad girl, you got me in it.
B7
A7
Boo-gie; a man could die for the way I'm think-ing, boo-gie child.

B7
A7
To Coda
G7
3 fr.
Boo-gie; and I'm in too deep and I just keep sink-ing. When you move it
A7
G7
3 fr.
like you real-ly know__ how to move me, I'll fol-low you wher-ev-er you go.__
D
C
G
D
C
I just wan-na lay__ my love on you.__ That boo-gie child, she can
B7
A7
B7
boo-gie.__ Ah, you sex-y, sex-y boo-gie child. Boo-gie;__ the sit-u-

A7
B7
a - tion___ wrecks_ me. Boo - gie;___ I___ can't stand_______
A7
B7
A7
the way you do it, boo-gie child. Boo-gie;_ bad girl, don't put me through this.
G7
3 fr.
A7
Boo-gie child, she's hon-ey sweet._ She's got hun-gry love;_
G7
3 fr.
D
C
it's good e - nough_ to eat.______ You can't touch her 'cause_ you know_

G
D
C
G
she's mine.
Come on, boo-gie child, let your love light shine.
D
C
G
D
C
I just wan-na lay my love on you.
That boo-gie child, she can.
No chord
F#7+9
8 fr.
N. C.
6
F7+9
7 fr.
F#7+9
8fr.
Gm
3 fr.
6
3
3
3

Bbm
C#m
4 fr.
A7
G#7
4 fr.
Tacet
B7
A7
B7
Boo-gie, ah you sex-y, sex-y boo-gie child. Boo-gie; the sit-u-
A7
B7
A7
a-tion wrecks me. Boo-gie; I can't stand the way you do it, boo-gie child.
B7
A7
D
C
Boo-gie; bad girl, don't put me through this. You can't touch her, 'cause you know

G
D
C
G
she's mine.
Come on, boo-gie child, let your love light shine.
D
C
G
D
C
D. S. al Coda
I just wan-na lay my love on you.
That boo-gie child, she can.
Coda
Eb7
E7
F7
F#7
G7
G#7
A7
Bb7
B7
C7
6fr.
3 fr.
4fr.
(spoken) just keep sink-ing.
Repeat and fade
B7
A7
Boo-gie, boo-gie child.
Come on, boo-gie, boo-gie.
Repeat and fade

COME ON OVER

Moderately

Words and Music by BARRY GIBB,
MAURICE GIBB and ROBIN GIBB

Tacet
mf
E
If my life gets like a jig - saw
A
E
B
with the piec - es out of place, come on o - ver,

E
put a smile — back on — my face. — And if
E
A
all my bad — days came at once you would know just what to
can-not see — in front of me and I know my dark-est
E
B
do. Come on o - ver; ba - by, you — will see — me through. —
day, come on o - ver; you can take — it all — a - way. —
E
A
B
E
And if — you think — I need — you, come on o -

A
E
G♯m
4 fr.
ver. Bring your love a - round; you can dry a - way my tears.
F♯m
B
A
B
And if you think I need you, come on o -
E
A
E
ver. Lay your bod - y down; you know
G♯m
4 fr.
F♯m
B
To Coda
I will be here. So bring your love a - round.

E
A
E
A
D. S. 𝄋 al Coda 𝄌
When I
Coda 𝄌
E
A
E
A
E
Come on o -
A
E
ver
here.
rit.

EDGE OF THE UNIVERSE

Words and Music by BARRY GIBB,
MAURICE GIBB and ROBIN GIBB

Moderately

D
G/D
Em
Now I look out on for - ev -
F♯m
Em
A
er and it must be nice down there.
And they call
Em
A
To Coda
D
me Shen - an - do - ra in the air.
G/D
D
G/D
Well, I'm ten feet tall, but I'm on - ly three feet wide.
est jour - ney and I've come through the black of night.

D
G/D
D
And I live inside an ocean that flows
I was tired and hungry when I
G/D
D
G/D
on the other side.
saw your distant light.
If I came
Well, I know
Em
F♯m
Em
back down to-morrow, would it all be far too soon?
this may sound crazy, but I'm sure I got here first.
A
Em
A
And it looks like it's gonna be a lovely afternoon.
I'm just me, Shenandora, at the edge of the universe.

D
G/D
B
I thought that I was go -
E
F#
B
E
F#
ing home, and all the way I kept on pray - in'.
B
E
F#
B
I could-n't stop to turn a - round; well, here I am and here
E
F#
G
I'm stay - in'.

A
1.
2.
D. S. al Coda
It's been my long -
Just my dog
Coda
D
Repeat and fade
D
At the edge of the u - ni - verse.
Repeat and fade
G/D
D
G/D
At the edge of the u - ni -

FANNY (BE TENDER WITH MY LOVE)

Words and Music by BARRY GIBB,
MAURICE GIBB and ROBIN GIBB

Moderately

C♯m B G♯ F♯m7 G♯7
4 fr.
sure been a lone - ly time right up to the time I met
start of a love af - fair the mo - ment when I first met
C♯m7 C♯m B G♯
you. So if you take a love like mine
you. And if you want I'll take you there;
be ten -
Amaj7 G♯m7 F♯m7 G♯7
der with my love; you know how eas - y it is to hurt
break
C♯m7 Amaj7 G♯m7
me. Fan - ny, be ten - der with my love, 'cause it's all

F♯m7
B11
1.
— that I've got — and my love — won't { de - sert — / for - sake — } me.
So you
2.
Tacet
A
With my — love,
G♯m
4 fr.
A
our love will seal it - to - geth - er. Oh, with our — love,
B
D. S. 𝄋 and fade
you made - a prom - ise - you'll al - ways - love me — for - ev - er. Be ten -

FIRST OF MAY

Words and Music by BARRY GIBB,
MAURICE GIBB and ROBIN GIBB

F#m
G
D
A
passed us by; some-one else moved in from far a - way.
of them all, the day I kissed your cheek and you were gone.
Now
G
D
Em7
we are tall and Christ-mas trees are small, and you don't ask the time of
D
D7
G
D
day. But you and I, our love will nev - er die, but
Em7
G
1. D
A
2. D
D. S. 𝄋 (lyric 1) and fade
guess who'll cry come first of May. The May. When

HE'S A LIAR

Words and Music by BARRY GIBB,
MAURICE GIBB and ROBIN GIBB

Driving beat

Dm Am D G D
there in the dark and I saw you to - geth - er, you were up in his arms, I was down on my
Am D Am
knees. Get the cards on the ta - ble, no need to pre - tend, You've got to be cruel to be
D Am D C
Chorus
F G
kind. He can sell you his love and you know you will pay 'cause He's A Li - ar
F G A F#m D F G
He's A Li - ar And I should know Li - ar
cresc.
F G A F#m D Am
He's A Li - ar And I should know Ahh
cresc.
mf

cresc. poco a poco
Dm
Dm/C
Bm7-5
To Coda
Bb7
Dm
ff
dim.
Well they
C
Bb
Am
Bb
C
told me I fell but I just don't re - mem - ber. I was stand - ing face down, they were
mf

D Bm Am Dm C Bb Am
there at my feet. There was smoke in the air and the sweet smell of lea - ther, I was
D G D Am
out through the win - dow and down in the street. Well I'm cold and I'm hun - gry but
D Am D Am
I'm still a - live, And it's not how I want it to be. There's a hand on my shoul - der, he
D C
D.S. al Coda
said I'll sur - vive, but He's a
CODA
E7 A
Am D Am
Was it not for the man that was block - ing the drive, Was it not for the red lim - o -

D
Am
sine.
I'd be mil - lions of miles from the
D
Am
scene of the crime,
And some - how in this mad - ness be -
D
C
F
G
F
G
lieve she was mine. But I'm a li - ar
He's A
A
F#m
D
F
G
F
G
Li - ar And I should know li - ar.
He's A
A
F#m
D
D.S. and Fade
Li - ar and I should know Ahh
He's A

HOLIDAY

Words and Music by BARRY GIBB,
MAURICE GIBB and ROBIN GIBB

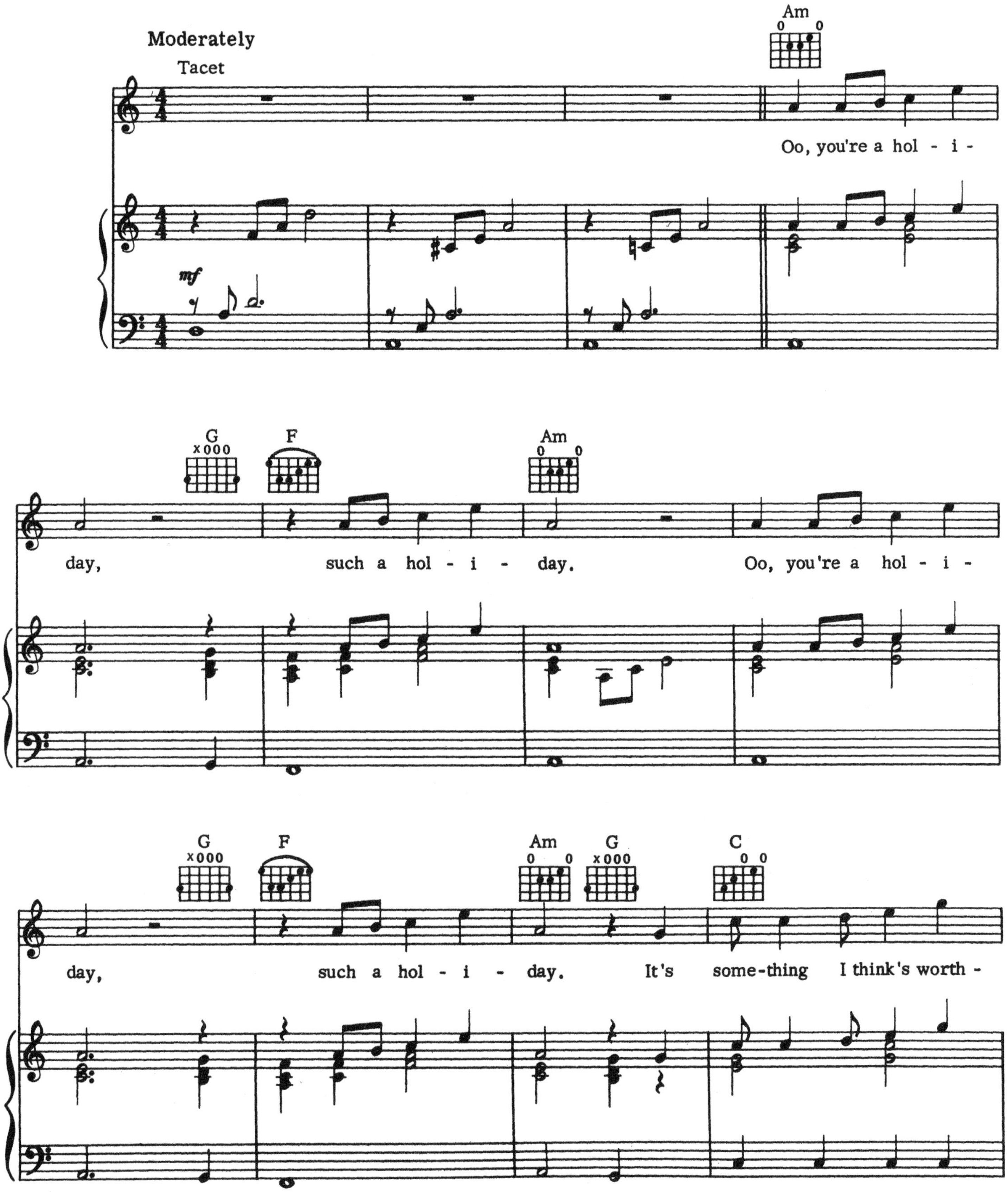

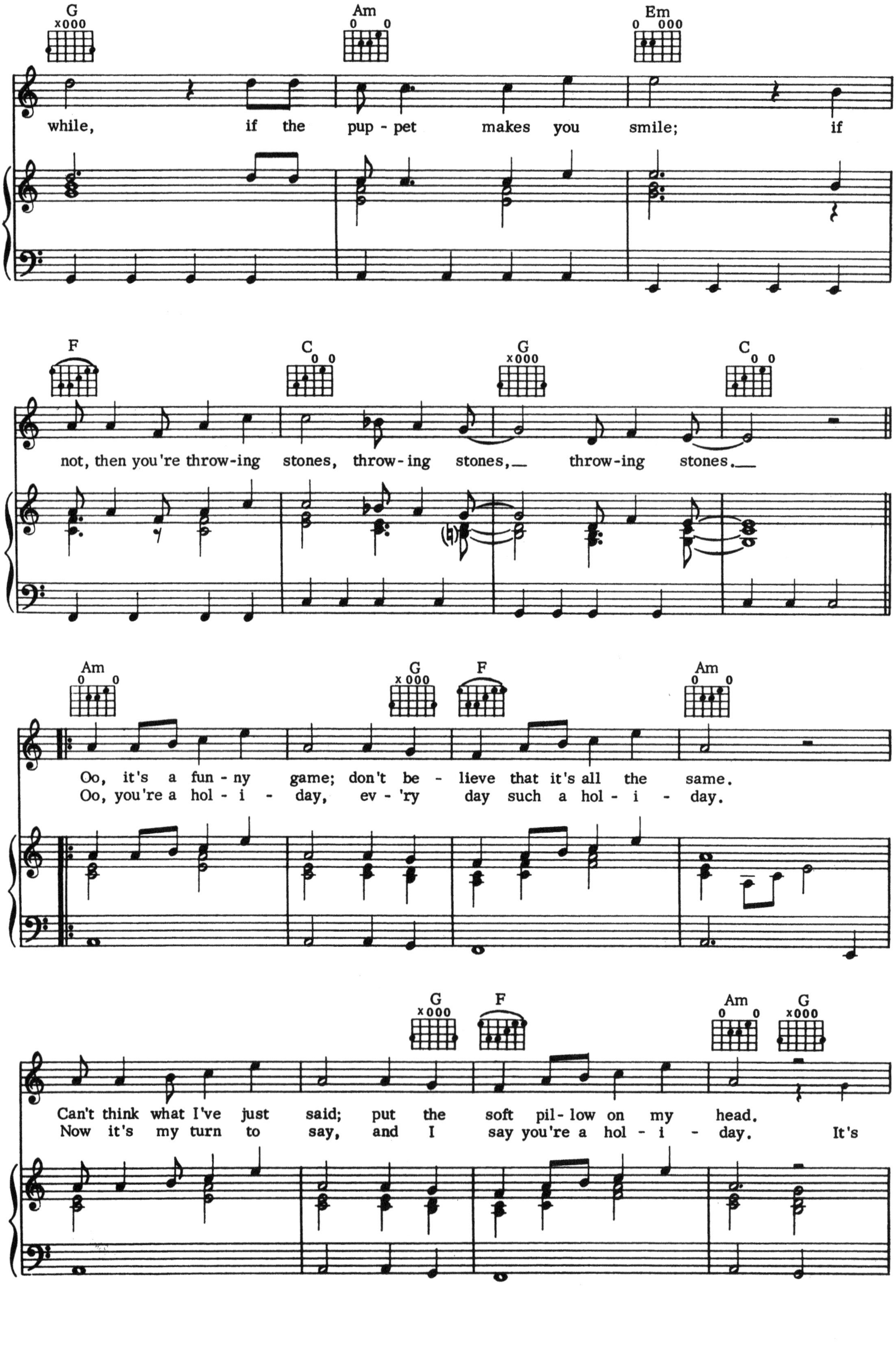
G
Am
Em
while, if the pup-pet makes you smile; if
F
C
G
C
not, then you're throw-ing stones, throw-ing stones, throw-ing stones.
Am
G
F
Am
Oo, it's a fun-ny game; don't be-lieve that it's all the same.
Oo, you're a hol-i-day, ev-'ry day such a hol-i-day.
G
F
Am
G
Can't think what I've just said; put the soft pil-low on my head.
Now it's my turn to say, and I say you're a hol-i-day. It's

C
G
Am
Em
Mil - lions of eyes can see, yet why am I so blind? When the
some - thing I think's worth - while, if the pup - pet makes you smile; if
F
C
G
C
some - one else is me, it's un - kind, it's un - kind,
not, then you're throw - ing stones, throw - ing stones, throw - ing stones.
Am
G
F
Am
Dee dee dee dee dee dee dee dee dee dee dee dee dee,
G
F
dee dee dee dee dee dee dee dee dee dee dee.

HOW CAN YOU MEND A BROKEN HEART

Words and Music by BARRY GIBB,
MAURICE GIBB and ROBIN GIBB

Slowly
Tacet
mp
E
Emaj7
I can think of young - er days when liv - ing for my life was
I can still feel the breeze that rus - tles through the trees and
F♯m7
E
G♯
4 fr.
ev - 'ry - thing a man could want to do. I could nev - er see to -
mist - y mem - o - ries of days gone by. We could nev - er see to -
mf

C#m
4 fr.
F#
B
mor - row, but I was nev-er told a - bout the sor - row.
mor - row; no one said a word a - bout the sor - row.
E maj7
mp
And how can you mend a bro-ken heart?
F#m7
A
B
How can you stop the rain from fall-ing down? How can you stop
A
B
F#m7
B
E
the sun from shin-ing? What makes the world go 'round?

E maj7
F♯m7
How can you mend this bro-ken man? How can a los-er ev-er
A
B
win? Please help me mend my bro - ken heart
F♯m7
B
1. E
and let me live a - gain.
2. E
E maj7
gain.
rit.

HOW DEEP IS YOUR LOVE

Words and Music by BARRY GIBB,
MAURICE GIBB and ROBIN GIBB

Moderately

Fm7
Ab/Bb
4 fr.
Abmaj7
4 fr.
feel you in my arms a - gain. And you come to me on a sum -
sav - ior when I fall. And you may not think I care
Gm7
3 fr.
Fm7
mer breeze; keep me warm in your love, then you soft -
for you when you know down in - side that I real -
Db9
3 fr.
Gm7
3 fr.
Ab/Bb
4 fr.
how deep is your love.
ly leave.
ly do.
And it's me you need to show:
How deep

Eb
Ebmaj7
Abmaj7
6 fr.
4 fr.
is your love? How deep is your love? I real-ly mean to learn.
Abm6
Eb
Bbm/Db
3 fr.
'Cause we're liv-ing in a world of fools, break-ing us
C7
Fm7
down when they all should let us be. We be-long
Abm6
Eb
Gm7
Ab/Bb
to you and me.
D. S. and fade
How deep

I CAN'T SEE NOBODY

Words and Music by BARRY GIBB,
MAURICE GIBB and ROBIN GIBB

Moderately

A
E
Em
3
feel - ing that po - sess - es me.
love you and that's all I can say.
I just can't
You're ev-'ry, ev - 'ry
D
A
E
move my - self. I guess it all just had to be.
breath that I take. You are my nights; my night and day.
A
D
E
A
D
E
I can't see no - bod - y. No, I can't see no - bod - y.
A
D
E
A
E
My eyes can on - ly look at you. You

Em
D
A
Ev-'ry sin-gle word you hear, girl, is com-ing from this
E
Em
D
heart of mine.
I nev-er felt like this be-fore; a
I lost you such a long time a-go.
A
E
To Coda
Em
love like yours, so young and fine.
Don't know why. Said I don't know why.
And now as I try
D
A
E
to for-get you, it does-n't work out an-y way.

Em
D
A
I lost you such a long time a - go. But in my heart, you'll
E
D.S. al Coda
Coda
al-ways stay.
Ba - by.
A
D
E
A
I can't see no - bod - y. No, I can't see
D
E
A
D
E
A
no - bod - y. My eyes can on - ly look at you.

I STARTED A JOKE

Words and Music by BARRY GIBB,
MAURICE GIBB and ROBIN GIBB

Moderately slow, in 2

G Bm C D
see that the joke was on
G Bm C D
me, oh, no.
G Bm C D
I start - ed to cry which start - ed the whole world
I fi - nal - ly died which start - ed the whole world
G Bm C D
laugh - ing;
liv - ing;
oh, if I'd on - ly

G
Bm
C
D
To Coda
seen that the joke was on
G
Em
me. I looked at the
cresc.
f
Bm
C
skies, run - ning my hands o - ver my
G
Bm
eyes; and I fell out of

Em
Em/D
Am
D
1.
bed, hurt - ing my head from things that I said. Till
mf
2.
D. S. 𝄋 (lyric 2)
al Coda
Till
mf
Coda
G
Bm
C
me, oh, no, that the
gradual cresc.
D
G
Bm
C
D
joke was on me,
G
Bm
C
D
G
oh.
f
mp

I'VE GOTTA GET A MESSAGE TO YOU

Words and Music by BARRY GIBB,
MAURICE GIBB and ROBIN GIBB

Cm
3 fr.
F
once in your life_ you're a - lone,
but you ain't got a dime,_ there's no
once in my life_ I'm a - lone,
and I got - ta let her know just in
cry-ing, but deep_ down in- side,
well, I did it to him,_ now it's
cresc.
G
C
time for the phone."_
time be - fore I go.
my turn to die._
I've just got - ta get a mes-sage to you;_
f
Dm
F
G
C
hold on,_ hold on._ One more hour and my life will be through;_
Dm
F
G
1.2. C
F
3. C
G
D. S. and fade
hold on, hold on._
Well, I
I've just

IF I CAN'T HAVE YOU

Words and Music by BARRY GIBB,
MAURICE GIBB and ROBIN GIBB

Medium Rock beat

Bb/F
F
— to be no chance — for me. My life would end. — And it
Bbm/F
F
C/F
Bb/F
just don't mat-ter how I cry, — my tears — of love a waste —
C/F
Bb
— of time. If I turn — a - way, — am I strong — e-nough to see it through? —
Gm7
3 fr.
Bb
C 11
— Go cra - zy is what I will do — if I can't have you.

Dm
C
I don't want___ no-bod-y, ba-by, if I
Am
Dm
can't have you, ah,___ ah,___ if I
C
can't have you. I don't want___ no-bod-y, ba-by, if I
Am
Dm
can't have you, ah,___ ah.___ Can't let

F
Bbm/F
F
C/F
go, and it does-n't mat-ter how I try. I gave
Bb/F
C/F
it all so eas-i-ly to you, my love, to dreams
Bb
Gm7
3 fr.
Bb
that nev-er will come true. Am I strong e-nough to see it through?
Gm7
3 fr.
Bb
C11
D. S. and fade
Go cra-zy is what I will do if I can't have you.

JIVE TALKIN'

Words and Music by BARRY GIBB,
MAURICE GIBB and ROBIN GIBB

Moderately, with a strong beat

Bb C G F
real - ly no good.
Oh, my child,
Oh, my love,
you'll nev - er know
you are so good,
E Am
just what you mean to me.
treat - ing me so cruel.
G F
Oh, my child,
There you go with your
you got so much;
fan - cy lies,
C Bb F G
you're gon - na take a - way my en - er - gy with all your
leav - in' me, look - in' like a dumb - struck fool with all your
C
jive talk - in', you're tell - in' me lies, yeah.
jive talk - in', you're tell - in' me lies, yeah.
Good lov - in', still
Jive talk - in', you

F
C
gets in my eyes.
wear a dis - guise.
No - bod - y be - lieves what you say; it's just your
Jive talk - in', so mis - un - der - stood, yeah;
B♭
C
C
jive talk - in' that gets in the way.
jive talk - in', you just ain't no good.
Love talk - in' is
F
C
all ver - y fine, yeah; jive talk - in' just is - n't a crime. And if there's
some - bod - y you'll love till you die, then all that jive talk - in' just

Bb
C
No chord
gets in your eye.
Do be lu bu loop do be lu bu loop
do do do do doot doot, do be lu bu loop do be lu bu loop
Repeat and fade
C
do doot do. Jive talk - in'
Repeat and fade

JUMBO

Words and Music by BARRY GIBB,
MAURICE GIBB and ROBIN GIBB

F
G
x000
B♭
climb a moun - tain, sail a sail - boat through a
hes - i - ta - tion. There will be no rec - re -
A
0 0
D
0
foun - tain.
a - tion.
Jum - bo said to say good - night, and
he's a friend of yours.
D
0
Lis - ten to the tune; and if it's loud, it's up to you. It's on - ly

Dsus4
sound - er than a spar - row, and it shoots a bow 'n' ar - row through a
D7
song that's like a pow - der with a gun that's e - ven loud - er. And it's
G/D
sad e - nough to hear you must - a lis - ten with your ear in or - der to
D7
get to you.
Repeat and fade
D7
Repeat and fade

LIVING EYES

Words and Music by BARRY GIBB,
MAURICE GIBB and ROBIN GIBB

Moderate Rock

f
mf
8va
Dm
Bb
Would you be-lieve me if I told you your to-mor-row is my
Dm
F
yes-ter-day? But be a-live I know that we will The
E
F
Dm
world keeps on mov-in' but I'm hold-in' still.
In the be-gin-ning I was
When I been o-ver I been
(mf)

Bb Dm F
far a-way and pray-ing for my des-ti-ny that would ar-rive the mo-ment
un-der I don't own a dream to an-a-lyse But Liv-in' Eyes you know that
E F
you're born For we will be here when the mir-a-cle comes. Liv-ing
I do Be-lieve in the soul and the ma-gic of you. Liv-ing
A D A
Eyes when un-der the sun don't cry No
f
D Dm A
war in my mind the state of my heart Liv-ing Eyes when
D A D
out in the rain will fall The day I de-ny the

Dm
Bb
F
face of my love We are of age we are in time we are for - ev - er Right
Gm
Dm
Bb
now when the pow - er is mine I leave you hea-ven and the earth I leave you
F
Gm
A
Dm
To Coda
nev - er And liv - in' to love is the rea - son we shine
ff
D.S. al Coda
CODA
Bb
Eb
Liv-ing Eyes when un - der the sun don't
f
Bb
Eb
Ebm
Repeat and Fade
cry No war in my mind the state of my heart Liv-ing

LONELY DAYS

Words and Music by BARRY GIBB,
MAURICE GIBB and ROBIN GIBB

2
B♭
Bdim
Cm
Ah.
Faster
Moderate Rock
C
B♭
F
B♭
Lone - ly days,
lone - ly nights,
where would I be with - out my
C
B♭
F
wom - an?
Lone - ly days,
lone - ly nights,

1
C
B♭
F
Where would I be with-out my wom-an?
2
B♭
C
Cm
Slowly
where would I be with-out my wom-an?
Lone-ly days,
F
B♭
Cm
lone-ly nights,
where would I be with-out my wom-an?

LOVE SO RIGHT

Words and Music by BARRY GIBB,
MAURICE GIBB and ROBIN GIBB

Amaj7
G♯m7
4 fr.
F♯m7
Emaj7
lov - ing me. And I thought I'd found the heav - en in her eyes. But the
F♯m7
B7
G♯7
4 fr.
C♯m
4 fr.
morn - ing when I woke up, I was here and she was gone; now I'm
F♯m7
F♯m7/B
hang - ing on. May - be you can tell me how a
cresc.
Amaj7
G♯m7
4 fr.
C♯m7
4 fr.
F♯m7
love so right can turn out to be so wrong, oh, my dar -
mf

F♯m7/B
Amaj7
G♯m7
4 fr.
C♯m7
4 fr.
ling. How a love so right can turn out to be so wrong.
F♯m7
F♯m7/B
E
F♯m7
Where did she go when I need her
dim.
mp
Amaj7
G♯m7
4 fr.
F♯m7
Emaj7
close to me? And the per-fect sto-ry end-ed at the start. I
F♯m7
B7
G♯7
4 fr.
C♯m
4 fr.
thought you came for-ev-er, and you came to break my heart. Now I'm

F#m7
F#m7/B
hang-ing on on the chance that you'll come back to me. How a
cresc.
Amaj7
G#m7
4 fr.
C#m7
4 fr.
F#m7
love so right can turn out to be so wrong, oh, my dar-
mf
F#m7/B
Amaj7
G#m7
4 fr.
C#m7
4 fr.
ling. How a love so right can turn out to be so wrong,
F#m7
F#m7/B
A
oh, my dar - ling. I could take it in my stride, start

Am
G♯m7
4 fr.
liv - ing for the mo - ment. May - be half the things_ we sought were
C♯7
4 fr.
F♯m7
nev - er there. Sim - ply o - pen up our eyes and break it down to size. It
Repeat and fade
F♯m7/B
Amaj7
G♯m7
4 fr.
is - n't real - ly fair ______ how a love so right can
Repeat and fade
C♯m7
4 fr.
F♯m7
F♯m7/B
turn out to be so wrong, ____ oh, my dar - ling. How ____ a

LOVE YOU INSIDE OUT

Words and Music by BARRY GIBB,
MAURICE GIBB and ROBIN GIBB

Am7
B7
cheat - in', and the pain grows in - side me; it's e - nough to leave me
Em9
A7sus4
cry - ing in the rain.
Love you for - ev - er but you're
Dmaj7
B7(♭9)
driv - ing me in - sane and I'm hang - ing on.
Oh,
Em9
Oh, I'll win, I'll nev - er give in, our love has got the pow - er,
Wrap my - self up and take me home a - gain,

too man - y lov - ers in one life - time ain't good for you.
too man - y heart - aches in one life - time ain't good for me.
Dmaj7
Am7
You treat me like a vi - sion in the night, some - one
I fig - ure it's the love that keeps you warm, let this
B7
Em7
there to stand be - hind you when your world ain't work - in' right.
mo - ment be for - ev - er we won't ev - er feel the storm.
A7sus4
Em7
A7
Em7
F♯m7
I ain't no vi - sion, I'm the man who loves you

Bm7
A7sus4
Dmaj7
in - side and out,
back-wards and for - wards with my heart hang - ing out.
Em7
F#m7
Bm7
Em7
I love no oth - er way.
What am I gon - na do if we
A7sus4
D7
lose that fire?
Don't try to tell me it's all o - ver,
I can't hear a word, I can't hear a line.

No man could love you more_ and that's what I'm cry - in' for.__
You can't change the way_ I feel_ in - side._
G
You are the rea - son for my
F
laugh - ter and my sor - row,_
Em7
Blow out the can - dle I will
A7
burn a - gain to - mor - row.__
Dmaj7
No man on earth_ can stand be - tween my
Am7
love and I, and no

B7
Em9
A7sus4
mat-ter how you hurt_ me I will love you till I die._ I ain't no vi - sion, I'm the
Repeat and fade
Em7
A7
Em7
F#m7
Bm7
man who loves you in - side and out,__
A7sus4
Dmaj7
Em7
F#m7
back-wards and for - wards with my heart hang - ing out._ I love
Bm7
Em7
A7sus4
no oth - er way._ What am I gon - na do if we lose that fire?_____

MASSACHUSETTS
(THE LIGHTS WENT OUT)

Words and Music by BARRY GIBB,
MAURICE GIBB and ROBIN GIBB

G
home. And the lights all went out in Mas - sa -
do. And the lights all went out in Mas - sa -
seen. And the lights all went out in Mas - sa -
C
G
chu - setts the day I left her
chu - setts; they brought me back to
chu - setts; and Mas - sa - chu - setts is
D
G
1. 2.
D
3.
Am
C
stand - ing on her own.
see my way with you.
one place I have seen.
Repeat and fade
G
Am
C
G
Am
C
I will re - mem - ber Mas - sa - chu - setts.
Repeat and fade

MORE THAN A WOMAN

Medium Disco beat

Words and Music by BARRY GIBB,
MAURICE GIBB and ROBIN GIBB

Dbmaj7
4 fr.
Bb/C
Oh.
3
3
mf
Fmaj7
Girl, I've known you ver - y well. I've seen you grow - in' ev - 'ry day. I nev -
There are sto - ries old and true of peo - ple so in love like you and me,
Bb/C
er real - ly looked be - fore, but now you take my breath a - way.
and I can see my - self let his - to - ry re - peat it - self. Re -

Fmaj7
Sud - den - ly__ you're in__ my life,__ part of ev - 'ry - thing_ I do. You
flect - ing how_ I feel_ for you,__ think - in' 'bout_ those peo - ple then, I
B♭/C
got me work - ing day__ and night just tryin' to keep a hold__ on you.__
know that in__ a thou - sand years I'd fall in love with you__ a - gain.__
A♭
B♭
E♭maj7
Cm
Here in your arms__ I found__ my par - a - dise,
This is the on - ly way__ that we should_ fly.
A♭
B♭
Gm
my on - ly chance__ for hap - pi - ness.
This is the on - ly way to go.

Ab
4 fr.
Bb
Ebmaj7
Cm
3 fr.
And if I lose you now, I think I would die.
And if I lose your love, I know I would die.
Oh,
Dbmaj7
4 fr.
say you'll al - ways be my ba - by We can make it shine.
Bb/C
We can take for - ev - er just a min - ute at a time.
Oh.
Dbmaj7
4 fr.
More than a wom - an.
Ab
4 fr.
More than a wom - an to me.

Bbm
Dbmaj7
4 fr.
More than a wom - an.
Ab
4 fr.
Bbm
Dbmaj7
4 fr.
More than a wom-an to me.
3
3
Bb/C
Repeat and fade
Dbmaj7
4 fr.
Oh.
More than a wom - an
Repeat and fade
Ab
4 fr.
Bbm
More than a wom-an to me.

MR. NATURAL

Words and Music by BARRY GIBB,
MAURICE GIBB and ROBIN GIBB

Medium beat

Rust - y rain - bows. That's how the pain goes,
I went home laugh - ing, and in - side I'm cry - ing.
Dm/C
G
turn-ing me in - side out. Well, I come home at night and you are
We had a spe - cial thing. You know I loved you so much. But, girl, I'm
F
out of my sight. Yes, I'm dy - ing and there ain't no doubt.
so out of touch with my heart, and it won't sing.
C
Dm7
F
C
Well, I'm dy - ing and there's no way out.
You know my heart just won't sing.

C
Dm7
Well, I try, try, try, try, try. Mis-ter Nat-
C
Dm7
F
u-ral. (Come on, ba - by.) When I walk in the rain, you won't know
G
A
that I'm cry - ing: a smile on my face. And I'm try - ing, I'm
F
C
F
try-ing to un - der - stand that a love that is lost can

Fm
Em7
Am7
nev - er be found a - gain.
And you can
F
1. G7
C
see me dance. I look like a hap - py man.
2. G7
F
look like a hap - py man.
Still, I try,
Repeat and fade
C
Dm7
C
Dm7
try, try, try, try.
Mis-ter Nat - u-ral. (Come on, ba - by.) Well, I try,
Repeat and fade

MY WORLD

Words and Music by BARRY GIBB,
MAURICE GIBB and ROBIN GIBB

Chorus
A
Bm
My World is our world and this world is
E7
A
your world and your world is My World and
Bm
E7
E11
E7
A
My World is your world is mine.
Verse
A
C#m7
4 fr.
2. I've been cry - ing, I'm lone - ly. What
mf
mp

Bm7
E7
A
do I do to have you to stay.
I've need - ed you to
C♯m7
4fr.
Bm7
E7
cry on, I've writ-ten to you near-ly ev - 'ry day.
Chorus
A
Bm
E7
My World is our world and this world is your world and
mf
A
Bm
your world is My World and My World is

1
E7
A
your world is mine.
2.
F#7
B
Repeat and fade
your world.
My World is our world and
f Repeat and fade
C#m
4fr.
F#7
B
this world is your world and your world is
C#m
4 fr.
F#7
C#m7
4 fr.
F#7
My World and My World is your world is

MELODY FAIR

Words and Music by BARRY GIBB,
MAURICE GIBB and ROBIN GIBB

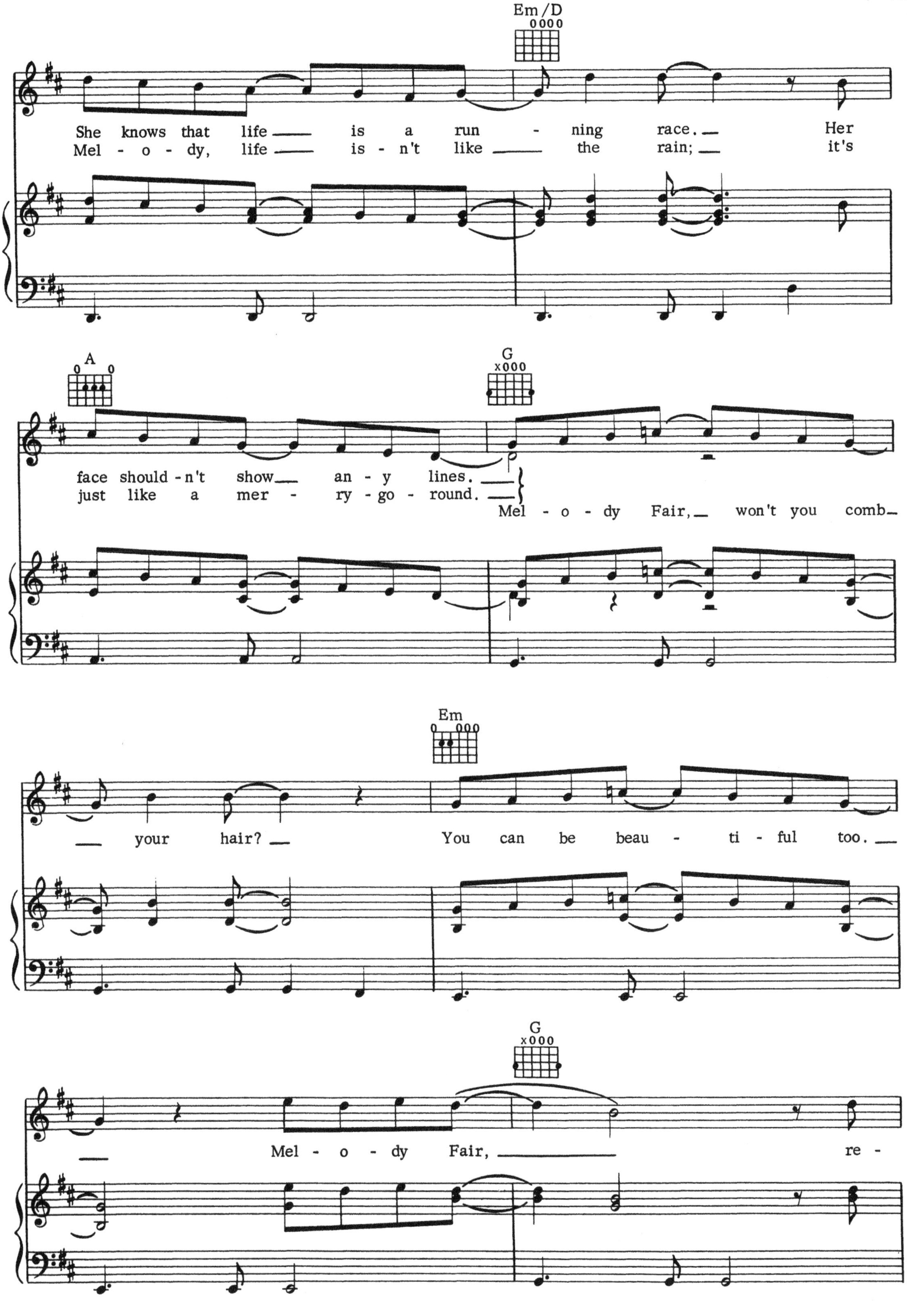
Em/D
She knows that life is a run - ning race. Her
Mel - o - dy, life is - n't like the rain; it's
A
G
face should - n't show an - y lines.
just like a mer - ry - go - round.
Mel - o - dy Fair, won't you comb
Em
your hair? You can be beau - ti - ful too.
G
Mel - o - dy Fair, re -

D
mem - ber you're on - ly a wom - an.
G
Mel - o - dy Fair, re -
D
mem-ber you're on - ly a girl.
1. Em7/A
Ah.
2. Em7/A
Ah.
D. S. 𝄋 (lyric 1) and fade

NEW YORK MINING DISASTER 1941

Words and Music by BARRY GIBB,
MAURICE GIBB and ROBIN GIBB

G
C
F
Jones? Do you know what it's like on the out - side? Don't go
E
To Coda
Am
talk - ing too loud, you'll cause a land - slide, Mis - ter Jones.
mp
Am
I keep strain - ing my ears to hear a sound; may - be
D7
G
some - one is dig-ging un - der - ground. Or have they giv - en up and all gone home to

Am D7 G F
bed thinking those who once existed must be dead? Have you
G C G C
seen my wife, Mister Jones? Do you know what it's like on the
mf
F E
outside? Don't go talking too loud, you'll cause a landslide, Mister
Am
Jones. In the e-
D. S. al Coda
Coda
Am Am/D
Jones.
mp

NIGHTS ON BROADWAY

Words and Music by BARRY GIBB,
MAURICE GIBB and ROBIN GIBB

Moderately slow (in 2), with a strong beat

Am
stran - gers,
oth - ers
Dm
stand - ing in the dark where your eyes could-n't
stand - ing in the line; how long will they stand be -
Am
see me.
tween us?
Well, I have to
Bb
fol - low you
Bbm
though you did not

F
want me to. But that won't stop my
Gm
3 fr.
lov - in' you; I can't stay a -
A
F
way. Blam - in' it all on the nights on
cresc.
f
Am
Bb
Broad - way, sing - in' them love songs,

B♭m
sing-in' them straight - to - the - heart songs. Blam - in' it all
F
Am
on the nights on Broad - way,
sing-in' them
B♭
1.
B♭m
sweet sounds to that cra - zy, cra - zy town.
2.
B♭m
Now cra - zy, cra - zy town.
mf

Dm
No chord
Dm
mf
N.C.
Am
mp
I will wait,
Dm
F
e - ven if it takes for -
G
Em
ev - er; I will wait,

Am
G
F
e-ven if it takes a life - time. Some-how I feel in - side
C
you nev-er ev-er left my side. Make it like it
F
Am
was be - fore e - ven if it takes a life -
Am/G
Am/D
D. S. 𝄋 and fade
time, takes a life - time. Blam-in' it all
cresc.
f

NIGHT FEVER

Words and Music by BARRY GIBB,
MAURICE GIBB and ROBIN GIBB

Medium Rock beat

Dm
waves of the air, there is danc - in' out there. If it's
fire in my mind. I got high - er in my walk - in'. And I'm
F
B♭
C
some - thin' we can share, we can steal it.
glow - in' in the dark; I give you warn - in'.
And that
Am
B♭
sweet cit - y wom - an, she moves through the light, con -
Am
Em
trol - ling my mind and my soul. When you

Am
Dm
A
reach out for me, yeah, and the feel - in' is bright, then I get
Dm7
Gm7
3 fr.
night fe - ver, night fe - ver. We know how to do
Fmaj7
Gm7
3 fr.
it. Gim - me that
Dm7
Gm7
3 fr.
night fe - ver, night fe - ver. We know how to show

Fmaj7
Gm7
3 fr.
it.
G
Dm
G
Here I am, pray-in' for this mo-ment to last,
Dm
G
Dm
liv - in' on the mu - sic so fine, borne on the wind,
G
Dm
G
D (no 3rd)
mak - in' it mine.

Dm7
Gm7
3 fr.
Night fe - ver, night fe - ver.
We know how to do
it.
Fmaj7
Gim - me that
night fe - ver, night fe - ver.
We know how to show it.
1.
2.
D. S. 𝄋 and fade
In the
Gim - me that

ONE

Words and Music by BARRY GIBB,
MAURICE GIBB and ROBIN GIBB

C
Dm
you're not there.__ (Yeah) Just as__ my life fades to dark-ness
B♭
C
Dm
G
Am
you make me see__ the light.__ Show me that my search is ov-er I pay the
F
/G
C
price, I pay the price.__ Tell you some - day,__
G
F
C
ba - by you and I should be one,__ one.__ Do it

C
G
F
C
al - ways, bright-er than the eye can see, we hide the sun.
1.
F
The taste of love is sweet-er like hon-ey on the vine, like the
G
F
C
wind that feeds the fi-re, two souls be-come en-twined. Some - day
G
F
C
ba-by you and I should be one, one. (2.) So I'm
2.

Cadd9
Dm
Ah we are one, we are
Em
F
G
C
one. I will
3.
C
G
F
C
Tell you some - day, ba - by, you and I should be one, one.
Dm7sus4
Fadd9

VERSE 2:
So I'm standing 'round this corner
Tall enough to touch the New York sky, oh yes
My love is so blind
I just cannot hear or see the world go by, oh yes
Someone can love so completely
One kiss should break the seal
Truth can be stronger than fiction
This love is real
This love is real.

VERSE 3:
I will follow
Count on me, I'll never let you down, oh yes
My devotion
If love is an ocean I'll surely drown, oh yes
You'll be my only possession
I'll be a slave to you
We hold the power together
Just me and you
Just me and you.

(OUR LOVE) DON'T THROW IT ALL AWAY

Words and Music by BARRY GIBB,
MAURICE GIBB and ROBIN GIBB

Bb
Bb/C
F
Fmaj7
Gm7
3fr.
Bb/C
Dar-ling, I can't see me in your eyes.
F
Gm/F
Fmaj7
Bb/F
I hold you near, but you're so far a-way. And it's
C
Am7
Bb
Bb/C
los-ing you I can't be-lieve, to watch you leave and let this feel-ing die.
F
F7
Bb
Bo7
You a-lone are the liv-ing thing that keeps
mp

Am7
Dm7
Gm7
3fr.
Gm7/C
— me a - live, — and to - mor - row — if I'm here — with - out — your love, —
F
Cm7/F
B♭
B°7
— you know I can't sur - vive. — On - ly — my love — can raise — you high —
Am7
B♭
Dm7/G
— a - bove — it all. — Don't
mf
C
G/C
3fr.
B♭maj7
F
throw it all a - way, our love, — our love; — don't throw — it all a - way, our love. — Don't

C
G/C
3fr.
Bbmaj7
F
throw it all a-way, our love, our love; don't throw it all a-way, our love.
F7
Bb
Bbm
Am7
D
Gm7
Gm7/C
F
Am
Gm7
Bb/C
Gm/F
We can take the dark-ness and make it
p
Fmaj7
Bb/F
full of light.
But let your love flow back to me. How can

Am7 Bb Bb/C F F7
— you leave — and let — this feel - ing die? —
Bb B°7 Am7 Dm7
This hap-py room will be — a lone - ly place — when you — are gone, —
mp
Gm7 3fr. Gm7/C F Cm7/F
and I — won't e - ven have — your shoul - ders for the cry - ing on. —
Bb B°7 Am7 Bb Dm7/G
No oth - er wom - an's love — could be — as true. I'm beg-gin' you.

C
G/C
3fr.
Don't throw it all a-way, our love, our love; don't throw
mf
Bbmaj7
F
C
G/C
3fr.
it all a-way, our love. Don't throw it all a-way, our love, our love; don't throw
Bbmaj7
F
Eb/F
F
it all a-way, our love.
Bbmaj7
Gm7
3fr.
Bbmaj7
Gm7
3fr.
We changed the world; we made it ours to hold. But dreams are
f

Gm7/C
Fmaj7
Am7
D
made for those who real-ly try. This los-ing you is real,
Bm7
E7
Am7
Am7/D
but I still feel you here in - side. Don't
mf
Repeat and fade
G
D/G
Fmaj7
C
throw it all a-way, our love, our love; don't throw it all a-way, our love. Don't
Repeat and fade
G
D/G
Fmaj7
C
throw it all a-way, our love, our love; don't throw it all a-way, our love. Don't

RUN TO ME

Words and Music by BARRY GIBB,
MAURICE GIBB and ROBIN GIBB

Moderately slow, with a beat

E
A
G
o-pen up your eyes to love me, and let it be like they said it would be,
o-pen up your eyes to love me, and when you've got noth-ing to lose,
3
F♯m
D
me lov-ing you girl and you lov-ing me.
noth-ing to pay for and noth-ing to choose,
Bm
E
Am I un-wise to o-pen up your eyes to love
Am I un-wise to o-pen up your eyes to love
Chorus
A
C♯m
4 fr.
D
Dm
Run to me when-ev-er you're lone-ly, run to me if you need a shoul-der.
(me.)
f

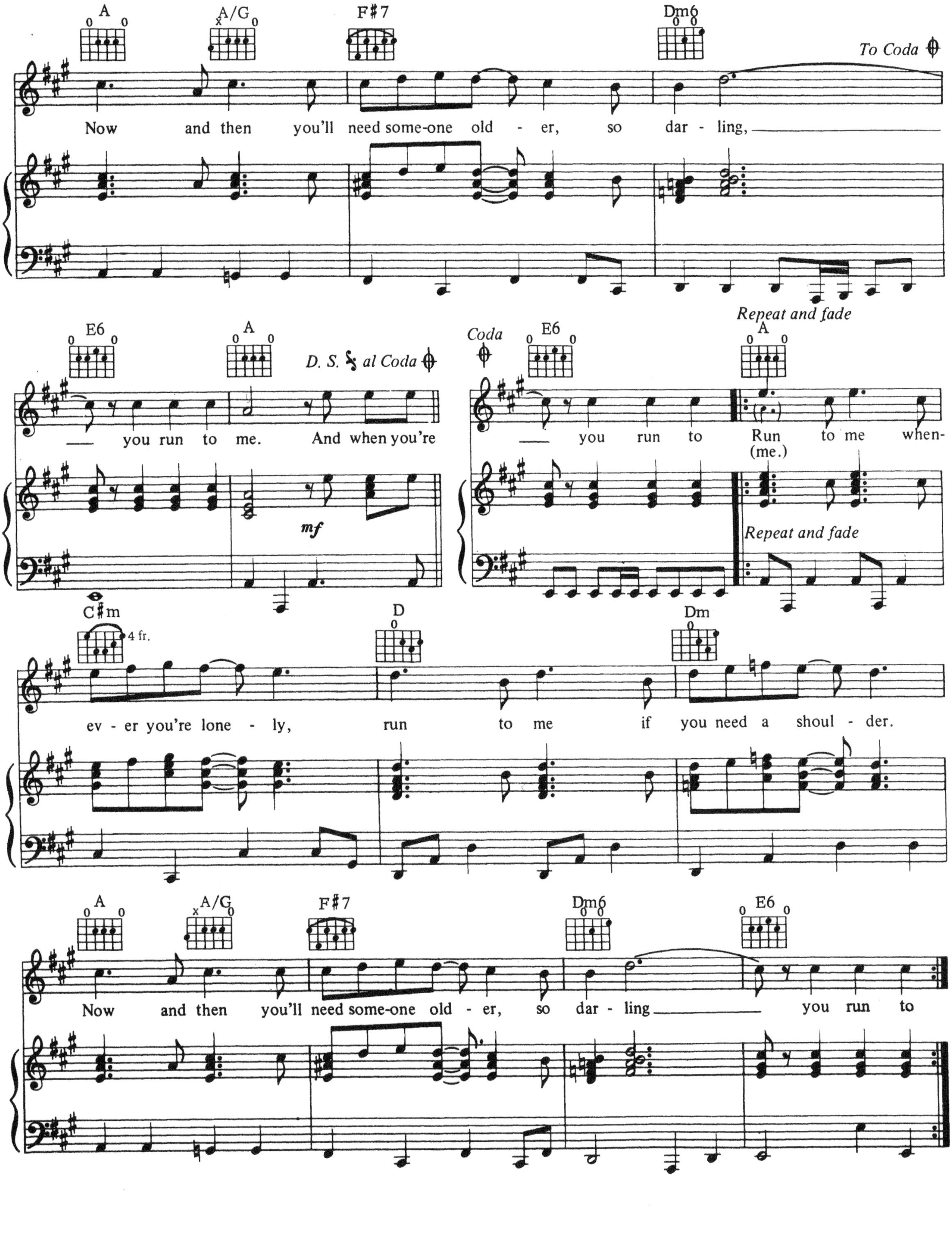
A
A/G
F#7
Dm6
To Coda
Now and then you'll need some-one old - er, so dar - ling,
E6
A
D. S. al Coda
you run to me. And when you're
mf
Coda
E6
Repeat and fade
A
you run to Run to me when-
(me.)
Repeat and fade
C#m
4 fr.
D
Dm
ev - er you're lone - ly, run to me if you need a shoul - der.
A
A/G
F#7
Dm6
E6
Now and then you'll need some-one old - er, so dar - ling you run to

SOMEONE BELONGING TO SOMEONE

Words and Music by BARRY GIBB,
MAURICE GIBB and ROBIN GIBB

Moderately Slow
mp
I know how__ I feel__
Fm
Cm7
lone - ly in the black of night; __ there can be no
can eat a - way a heart of stone, __ and ba - by if I

Fm
Cm
love for me now. No-bod-y lis-tens when the words ain't right, and you get in-to
leave you too late, it's just a feath-er and the bird has flown. It's cold-er when the
Bbm7
Eb
some-one else. It's hard for me to know who's lov-in' who and where do I stand..
fi-re dies. With all the trou-ble I'm in if I lose you too, then what is my life?
Ab
Cm
Fm
Cm
Fm
What did I do it all for? There's no one I could love more. I did it for your
If I don't wan-na go through an-y-thing with-out you, could-n't be a
mf
Bbm
Dbm
heart a-lone. All that I try to be, grow-in' in-side of me,
life at all. I could be ly-in' on, you are the on-ly one,

To Coda
Ab
Fm
I can be strong _ if you're there.
we did-n't make _ it by chance.
And there is some-one be-long-ing to some-one,
Cm
Bbm
Ab
Fm
Cm
and I got no one be-long-ing to me. ___
I,
I'm
Bbm
Dbm
Ab
Cm
live in a world _ where the face ___ of an an - gel is all ___ that a fool _ can see. _
caught in a world _ on the edge ___ of to-mor - row, it's all ___ that a fool _ can find. _
Bbm
Dbm
1 Ab
Gb
E
You got the pow - er to find _ me when-ev - er I'm _ lost.
I don't be-long _ in the arms _ of a love _ that is _
Where are you? _____ Who

D
Dbm
are we?
I be-lieve in time lost,
2 Ab
no-where to cry.
mp
Ped.
Cm
Gb
There must be some-thing we can say, my love, some-thing
Fm
Dbm
ex-cept good-bye.
D.S. al Coda (verse 2)
Oh what is my life?
CODA
Dbm
And there is
B
G#m
some-one be-long-ing to some-one,
D#m
C#m
B
G#m
D#m
C#m
and I got no one be-long-ing to me.
Repeat and Fade
And there is

THROW A PENNY

Words and Music by BARRY GIBB,
MAURICE GIBB and ROBIN GIBB

Moderately

G
D
G/D
D
new face__ star-ing right back__ at me.
vet day__ break-ing a - cross__ the sky.
I be - lieve,__ I am sure,__ that I'm tall -
I be - lieve,__ I am sure,__ that I'm tall -
F♯m
G
er than I was be - fore,__ build-ing a brand - new bridge__
er than I was be - fore,__ build-ing a brand - new bridge.__
D
in - to sin - cer - i - ty. But it's the
I know I'm gon - na try. But it's the

G
A
times like this — we must learn — to grow.
times like this — we must find — out why.
mf
D
G
Throw a pen - ny for my chil - dren. They — are go - ing down.
A
When the light — shines down much bright - er man - y souls —
D
— are found. — And I can't — be - lieve — what they're say -

G
ing in the o - ver-ground. Throw a pen -
A
To Coda
Bb
ny for my chil - dren go - ing down.
rit. e dim.
Slowly
Bb
Bb/Ab
Gm7
3 fr.
Lis - ten to the wise man as he breathes. He's real - ly lov - ing me.
mp
Cm7
3 fr.
Eb/F
Bb
He must be lov - ing me. At night I turn my

B♭/A♭
Gm7
3 fr.
face in - to the wind, and I whis - per se - cret - ly
Cm7
3 fr.
E♭/F
B♭
what means the most to me and bring him close.
G♭
D. S. 𝄋 al Coda ⊕
Tempo I
Tacet
Make it bad;
Coda
⊕
B♭
Repeat and fade
B♭
Throw a pen - ny for my chil - dren, for my chil - dren go - ing down.
Repeat and fade

STAYIN' ALIVE

Words and Music by BARRY GIBB,
MAURICE GIBB and ROBIN GIBB

Bb7
all right._ It's O K._ And you may look_ the oth - er way._
all right._ It's O K._ I'll live to see_ an - oth - er day._
We can try_ to un-der - stand_ the New York Times'_ ef - fect_ on man._
Fm7
Wheth-er you're a broth-er or wheth-er you're a moth-er, you're stay - in' a-live,_ stay-in' a-live._
Feel the cit-y break-in' and ev - 'ry-bod-y shak-in', and we're stay-in' a-live,_ stay-in' a-live._

Ah, ha, ha, ha, stay-in' a-live, stay-in' a-live. Ah, ha, ha, ha,
Fm
Eb/F
Fm
stay-in' a-live.
Cm7
3 fr.
To Coda
1.
Fm7
Well now, I
2.
Fm7
Bb7
Life go-in' no-where.

Fm7
Some-bod-y help me.
Some-bod - y help_ me, yeah.
B♭7
Life go - in' no - where.
Some-bod - y help_ me, yeah.
Fm7
D. S. 𝄋 (lyric 1) al Coda
Stay-in' a-live.
Well, you can tell
Coda
Fm7
Repeat and fade
B♭7
Life go-in' no - where.
Repeat and fade

Some-bod-y help me.
Some-bod - y help me, yeah.
Fm7
Bb7
Life go-in' no-where.
Some-bod - y help me, yeah.
Fm7
I'm stay-in' a-live.

TO LOVE SOMEBODY

Words and Music by BARRY GIBB,
MAURICE GIBB and ROBIN GIBB

Moderately

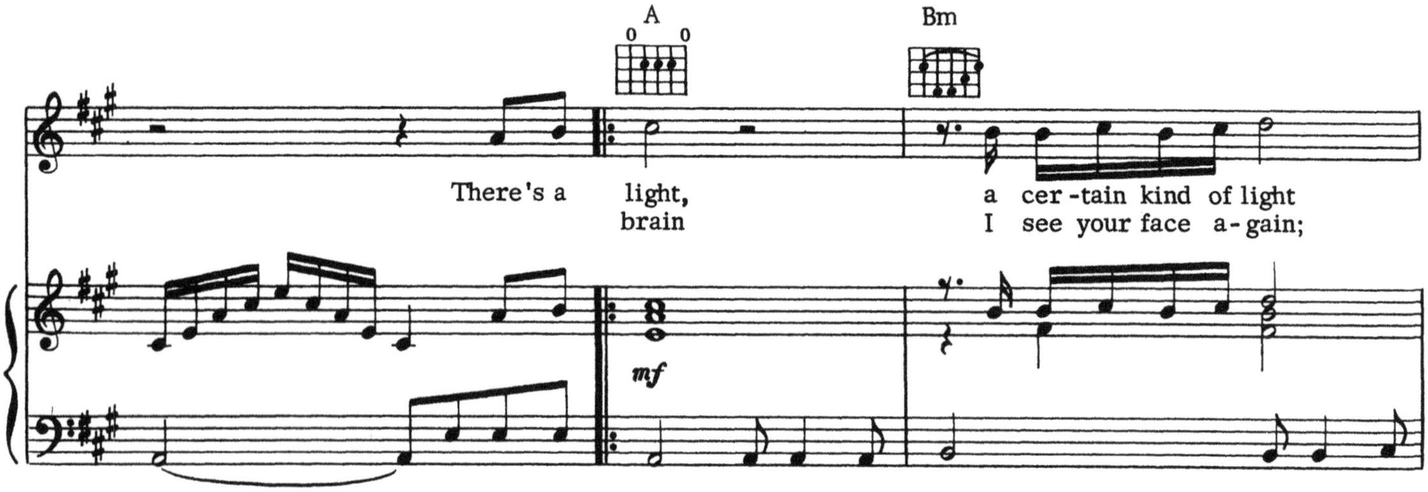

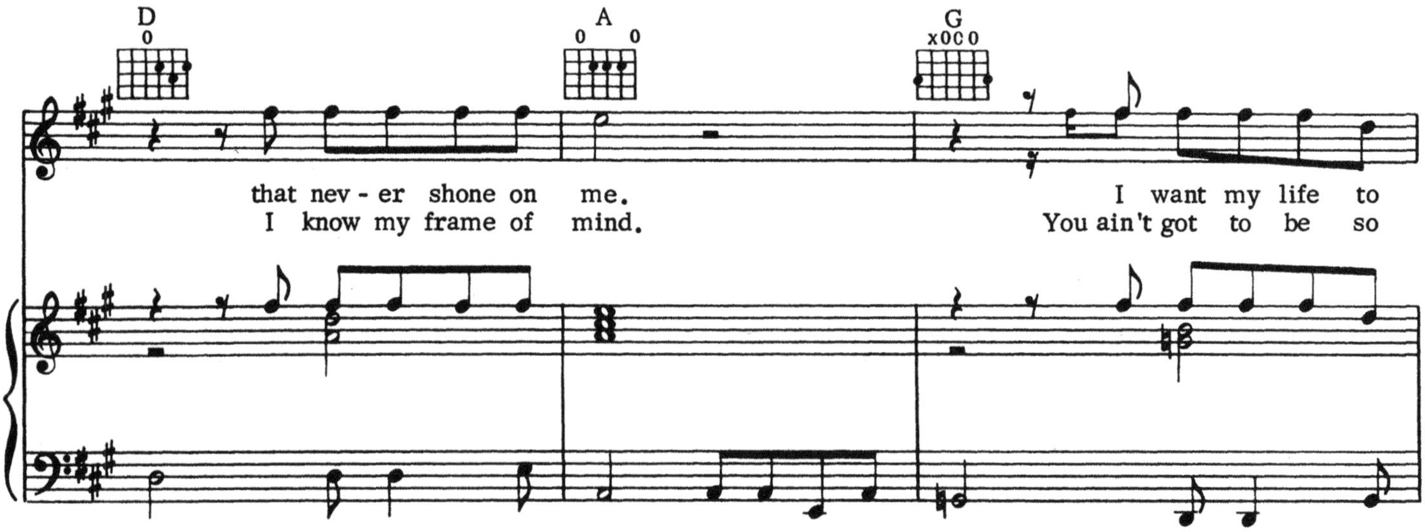

A
E
D7
be lived with you, lived with you. There's a
blind, and I'm blind, so ver - y blind. I'm a
A
Bm
way, ev - 'ry - bod - y say,
man, can't you see what I am?
D
A
to do each and ev - 'ry lit - tle thing.
I live and I breathe for you.
G
A
E
But what does it bring if I ain't got you, ain't got?
But what good does it do if I ain't got you, ain't got?

D7
A
E
You don't know what it's like, ba - by,
f
D
A
you don't know what it's like to love some -
E
D
bod - y, to love some - bod - y the way I
1.
A
2.
A
E
D. S. 𝄋 and fade
love you. In my love you.
decresc.

TRAGEDY

Words and Music by BARRY GIBB,
MAURICE GIBB and ROBIN GIBB

Moderate Disco tempo

mf
E♭
Here I lie in a lost and lone - ly part of town,
Night and day there's a burn - ing down in - side of me.

held in time in a world of tears I slow - ly drown.
Burn - ing love with a yearn - ing that won't let me be.
F
G
Go - in' home I just can't make it all a - lone, I
Down I go and I just can't take it all a - lone, I
F
real - ly should be hold - ing you, hold - ing you,
real - ly should be hold - ing you, hold - ing you,
A♭
4 fr.
lov - ing you, lov - ing you.
lov - ing you, lov - ing you.

Cm
Gm
Trag - e - dy, when the feel - ing's gone and you can't go on, it's
Cm
Gm
trag - e - dy; when the morn - ing cries and you don't know why, it's
B♭7sus4
Cm
hard to bear with no one to love you you're go - in' no - where.
A♭
4 fr.
G7
Cm
Gm
Trag - e - dy, when you lose con - trol and you got no soul, it's

Cm
Gm
trag - e - dy; when the morn - ing cries and you don't know why, it's
B♭7sus4
Cm
A♭
4 fr.
hard to bear with no one be - side you you're go - in' no - where.
G7
1. Cm
Fm7
Gm/D

Ab
4 fr.
Bb
Eb
Ebsus4
Eb/Bb
N.C.
2.
Cm
Fm7
G7
Cm

Fm7
G
A♭
4 fr.
A♭maj7
Repeat and fade
Cm
Gm
Trag - e - dy, when the feel - ing's gone and you can't go on, it's
Cm
Gm
trag - e - dy; when the morn - ing cries and you don't know why, it's
B♭7sus4
Cm
A♭
4 fr.
hard to bear with no one to love you, you're go - in' no - where.

G7
Cm
Gm
Trag - e - dy,
when you lose con - trol and you got no soul, it's
Cm
Gm
trag - e - dy;
when the morn - ing cries and your heart just dies, it's
B♭7sus4
3
hard to bear
with no one be - side you you're
Cm
A♭
4 fr.
G
go - in' no - where.
Oh.

TOO MUCH HEAVEN

Words and Music by BARRY GIBB,
MAURICE GIBB and ROBIN GIBB

Slow Ballad tempo

F#m7
Gmaj7
Dmaj7
A7sus4
love an - y more, it's as high as a moun - tain and hard - er to climb.
Oh, you and me, girl, got a lot of love in store, and it
Oh, you and me, girl, got a high - way to the sky, we can
flows through you and it flows through me and I love you so much more than my
turn a - way from the night and day and the tears we had to cry, you're my
Dmaj7
life. I can see be - yond for - ev - er, ev - 'ry - thing we are will nev - er
life. I can see a new to - mor - row, ev - 'ry - thing we are will nev - er

Gmaj7
G
A/G
F#m7
die. Lov - ing's such a beau - ti - ful thing,
die. Lov - ing's such a beau - ti - ful thing,
Bm7
A7sus4
oh, you make my world a sum - mer day, are you
when you are to me the light a - bove, there for
1.
2.
just a dream to fade a - way.
all to see our pre - cious love.
Dmaj7
F#m7
Gmaj7
No - bod - y gets too much heav - en no more; it's as high as a moun - tain and

Dmaj7
A7sus4
Dmaj7
hard - er to climb.
Oh,
Gmaj7
G
A/G
Oh, oh, oh.
Lov - ing's such a beau - ti - ful thing,
F#m7
A7sus4
oh, you make my world a sum - mer day, are you
C7sus4
just a dream to fade a - way.

Fmaj7
Am7
No - bod - y gets too much heav - en no more, it's much
Bbmaj7
Fmaj7
C7sus4
hard - er to come by; I'm wait - ing in line.
Fmaj7
Repeat and fade
Am7
No - bod - y gets too much love an - y more, it's as
Bbmaj7
Fmaj7
C7sus4
high as a moun - tain and hard - er to climb.

THE WOMAN IN YOU

Words and Music by BARRY GIBB,
MAURICE GIBB and ROBIN GIBB

fin - er parts of your a - na - to - my But ba - by
VERSE
Dm
Am
shar - per than a knife help me to know you Show me the night to
strong - er than the wind burn in the fire out of the night I'll
E7
sat - is - fy a sin - ner with the flash of an eye there'll nev - er be a - noth - er me
teach you how to trem - ble if you give me the night there'll nev - er be e - nough to me
To Coda
Am
I nev - er knew love could wind me up I don't do my stuff 'til you go
I nev - er knew I could find the best But search - in' out the rest there

walk-in' by and may-be old e-nough_ to try I nev-er knew a-ny-one in be-tween the
is no doubt and may-be we can sweat_ it out I nev-er knew we could find a way this
F#m
de-vil and the an-gel all in one and may-be old e-nough that I can ride your love_
cra-zy sit-u-a-tion o-ver me and we for-get a-bout the world out - side my love_
C#7
let me burn let me slide_ down_ to your soul_
in your eyes there's no world_ there_ is no time_
F#m
Dmaj7
E
you can pull_ me in you can push_ me out But your ba -
you can hold_ me in you can throw_ me down But your ba -

F
- by needs_ love some - bo - dy to hold show _ me what to do. The
- by needs_ love some - bo - dy to hold show _ me what to do. The
Am
wo - man in you brings out the man in me _ It's the
wo - man in you and the fin - er parts of your a - na - to - my.
8va basso
8va basso

D.S. al Coda
(Verse 2)
loco
loco
CODA
Am
The woman in you brings out the
man in me __ It's the woman in you and the
finer parts of your anatomy. The
Repeat and Fade

WORDS

Words and Music by BARRY GIBB,
MAURICE GIBB and ROBIN GIBB

Moderately slow
Tacet
mp legato
G
Smile an ev - er - last - ing smile; a smile could bring you
A
D
near to me. Don't ev - er let me find you

C G
gone 'cause that would bring a tear to me. This
B♭
world has lost its glo - ry; let's start a brand - new sto - ry
F G
now, my love. Right now, there'll be no oth - er
A D
time, and I can show you how, my love.

G
A
Talk in ev - er - last - ing words and ded - i - cate them all to me.
mf
D
And I will give you all my life, I'm here if you should
C
G
Bb
call to me. You think that I don't e - ven
D
Tacet
mean a sin - gle word I say. It's on - ly

G
D
words, and words are all I have to take your heart a -
G
D
Tacet
G
way. It's on - ly words, and words are all I
D
G
D
Tacet
have to take your heart a - way. It's on - ly
G
words, and words are all I have to take your heart a - way.
rit.
mp

WORLD

Words and Music by BARRY GIBB,
MAURICE GIBB and ROBIN GIBB

Moderately slow

Bm
G
F#m
Em
mor-row, where in the world will I be? To-
mem-ber all of the things I have done, I'd re-
Bm
G
F#m
Em
C
mor-row, how far am I a-ble to see?
mem-ber all of the times I've gone wrong.
G
F
Or am I need-ed here?
Why do they keep me here?
decresc.
G
A
D
Now I've found that the world is

Bm
G
A
round, and of course it rains ev - 'ry
1.
2.
D sus4
D
D sus4
A
day.
day.
And
cresc.
Repeat and fade
D
E
A
F♯m
now I've found that the world is round, and of
f
Repeat and fade
D
E
A sus4
A
course it rains ev-'ry day.
And

YOU STEPPED INTO MY LIFE

Words and Music by BARRY GIBB,
MAURICE GIBB and ROBIN GIBB

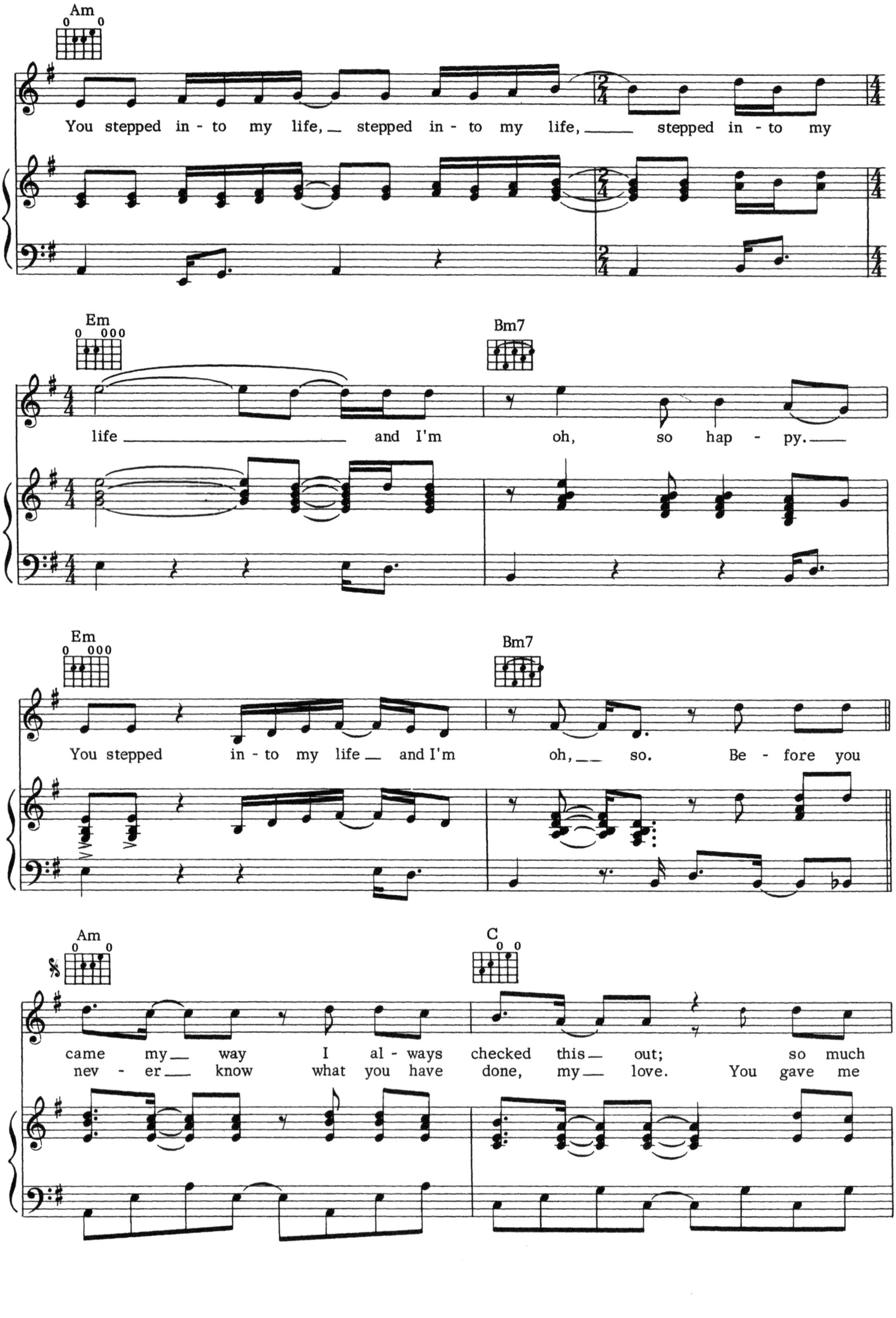
Am
You stepped in - to my life, stepped in - to my life, stepped in - to my
Em
Bm7
life and I'm oh, so hap - py.
Em
Bm7
You stepped in - to my life and I'm oh, so. Be - fore you
Am
C
came my way I al - ways checked this out; so much
nev - er know what you have done, my love. You gave me

B7
Em
pain in love and so a - lone in - side. I nev - er thought
so much more my love is wor - thy of. Be - neath my ver -
Am
C
that I'd be - lieve in love so much. But dar - ling
y soul I kneel be - fore your touch. Your touch is
B7
when you came close to me, sud - den - ly, sud - den - ly
ec - sta - sy, close to me. Sud - den - ly, sud - den - ly
Em
Bm7
you stepped in - to my life and I'm oh, so hap - py.

Em
Bm7
You stepped in - to my life and I'm oh, so hap - py.
Am
To Coda
Em
You stepped in - to my life, stepped in - to my life, stepped in - to my life.
Bm7
Em
C
Bm7
Em
C
Bm7
C

B7
Em
You stepped in - to my life _ and I'm
Bm7
Em
oh, __ so hap - py. You stepped in - to my life _ and I'm
Bm7
D. S. al Coda
Coda
Em7
oh, _ so. You will
life. ____
Repeat and fade
Am
Em7
Repeat and fade

YOU SHOULD BE DANCING

Moderately, with a beat

Words and Music by BARRY GIBB,
MAURICE GIBB and ROBIN GIBB

Tacet
mf
Gm
3 fr.
My ba - by moves at mid - night, goes
juic - y and she's trou - ble, she
right on till the dawn;
gets it to me good;
my wom - an takes me high - er,
my wom - an gives me pow - er,

my wom - an keeps me warm.
goes right down to my blood.
What you
Cm
Cm(maj7)
Cm7
Cm(maj7)
3 fr.
do - in' on your back,
aah,
what you
Cm
Cm(maj7)
Cm7
Cm(maj7)
Gm
do-in' on your back,
aah? You should be
danc - in', yeah,
1.
danc - in', yeah.
She's

2.
Cm
3 fr.
Cm(maj7)
What you do-in' on your back,
Cm7
Cm(maj7)
Cm
Cm(maj7)
what you do-in' on your back,
Cm7
Cm(maj7)
Gm
aah? You should be danc-in', yeah,
To Coda
danc-in', yeah.

Gm
3 fr.
Am
Gm
3 fr.
Am
Gm
3 fr.
D. S. 𝄋
(lyric 1–no repeats)
al Coda
My
Coda

About The Songs...

ALIVE
(B. & M. Gibb)

Recorded October 1972. Released as a single November 1972, from the album "To Whom It May Concern," released October 1972.

"It may seem strange to some that there are quite a few songs we don't remember writing. This is one of them."

Barry Gibb

BOOGIE CHILD
(B., R. & M. Gibb)

Recorded January 1976. Released as a single January 1977. From the album "Children Of The World," released September 1976.

"From the CHILDREN OF THE WORLD album, recorded at Criteria Studios in North Miami. The days when we were discovering probably one of the finest studios in America. Thanks Mack."

Maurice Gibb

EDGE OF THE UNIVERSE (LIVE VERSION)
(B. & R. Gibb)

Recorded December 1976. Released as a single June 1977. From the album "Here At Last...Bee Gees...Live," released June 1977.

"A humorous flight of fancy about an alien and his pet dog; baffling really."

Barry Gibb

FANNY (BE TENDER WITH MY LOVE)
(B., R. & M. Gibb)

Recorded January 1975. Released as a single January 1976. From the album "Main Course," released June 1975.

"Without a doubt one of the best R&B songs we ever wrote. I love Arif Mardin's production and his understanding from three brothers who love R&B. This one's for you Arif."

Maurice Gibb

FIRST OF MAY
(B., R. & M. Gibb)

Recorded August 1968. Originally released as a single February 1969. From the album "Odessa," released March 1969.

"Barnaby's birthday. When Linda and I first moved into an apartment near St. Paul's Cathedral, we got ourselves a Pyranian mountain dog and named him Barnaby. The idea came from then. Sad to say, Barnaby's gone but the song lives on."

Barry Gibb

HE'S A LIAR
(B., R. & M. Gibb)

Recorded 1981. Originally released as a single September 1981. From the album "Living Eyes," released October 1981.

"This piece of work raises more questions than answers."

Barry Gibb

HOLIDAY
(R. & B. Gibb)

Recorded April 1967. Released as a single (US) September 1967. From the album "Bee Gees 1st," released July 1967.

"Humble roots to be sure. This was written in Hendon, a leafy, lush suburb of London. One autoharp (zither) and three brothers."

Robin Gibb

HOW CAN YOU MEND A BROKEN HEART
(B. & R. Gibb)

Recorded January 1971. Originally released as a single June 1971. From the album "Trafalgar," released November 1971.

"Fifteen months after we broke up, Robin dropped into my place in Kensington. It was a cold, wet day and this song was born. We finished it with Mo, and the Bee Gees were reborn."

Barry Gibb

HOW DEEP IS YOUR LOVE
(B., R. & M. Gibb)

Recorded Spring 1977. Originally released as a single September 1977. From the album "Saturday Night Fever," released November 1977.

"Alot of mixed emotions about this one. We were accused of stealing it. One of the songs from FEVER. I would never have called it a disco song but there you have it."

Barry Gibb

I CAN'T SEE NOBODY
(R. & B. Gibb)

Recorded March 1967. Originally Released as the B-side of "New York Mining Disaster 1941" April 1967. From the album "Bee Gees 1st," released July 1967.

"The B-side of our first US single (1967) on ATCO and still one of my personal favourites. Influenced by the Soul stable of ATLANTIC and STAX, both lyrics and music were written in the basement of a seedy niteclub in Brisbane. That's why, even now, when I hear it today, it still manages to bring a lump."

Robin Gibb

I STARTED A JOKE
(B., R. & M. Gibb)

Recorded June 1968. Released as a single December 1968. From the album "Idea," released September 1968.

"The melody to this one was heard aboard a British Airways Vickers Viscount about a hundred miles from Essen. It was one of those old four engine 'prop' jobs, that seemed to drone the passenger into a sort of hypnotic trance, only with this it was different. The droning, after a while, appeared to take the form of a tune, which mysteriously sounded like a church choir. So it was decided! We accosted the pilot, forced him to land in the nearest village and there, in a small pub, we finished the lyrics. Actually it wasn't a village, it was a city, and it wasn't a pub, it was a hotel, and we didn't force the pilot to land in a field...but why ruin a perfectly good story?"

Robin Gibb

I'VE GOTTA GET A MESSAGE TO YOU
(B., R. & M. Gibb)

Recorded July 1968. Originally released as a single July 1968. From the album "Idea," released September 1968.

"Question...How do you arouse public interest in world events? Answer...Take a guy who's just about to be fried and turn it into a social statement.

Putting a strong theme into a 'pop' record and keeping it simple and commercial like this is never easy. 'Man pleading for his lover just before the switch is thrown, whilst confessing his guilt at the same time' – not exactly Oscar Wilde, but it had the desired effect."

Robin Gibb

IF I CAN'T HAVE YOU
(B., R. & M. Gibb)

Recorded Spring 1977. Released as the B-side of "Stayin' Alive," released December 1977. From the album "Bee Gees Greatest," released October 1979.

"Would you believe originally written for ABBA on the steps of the Chateau Studios in France. (Disco was K.C. and Donna.)"

Maurice Gibb

JIVE TALKIN'
(B., R. & M. Gibb)

Recorded January 1975. Originally released as a single May 1975. From the album "Main Course," released June 1975.

"Working with Arif immediately comes to mind. To be a great producer you should listen to the best and study the best, and I believe that as good as I may become, I will still be a student of Arif Mardin."

Barry Gibb

JUMBO
(B., R. & M. Gibb)

Recorded January 1968. Originally released as a single March 1968.

"Mo playing the Beatles Mellotron; a very experimental period. I think it's about a child's fantasy elephant, but when I listen again there are some very phallic overtones. Personally, I think THE SINGER SANG HIS SONG, the flip side, was a much stronger A-side."

Barry Gibb

LONELY DAYS
(B,. R. & M. Gibb)

Recorded October 1970. Originally released as a single November 1970. From the album "Two Years On," released December 1970.

"I started playing the piano and the three of us began to create our first number one in America. The same night we recorded HOW CAN YOU MEND A BROKEN HEART, our second number one – thank you America."

Maurice Gibb

LOVE SO RIGHT
(B., R. & M. Gibb)

Recorded January 1976. Released as a single September 1976. From the album "Children Of The World," released September 1976.

"One of my first attempts at falsetto lead. Tamla/Motown has always been a source of inspiration to us and this song is obviously drawn from our love of that music."

Barry Gibb

LOVE YOU INSIDE OUT
(B., R. & M. Gibb)

Recorded March-November 1978. Released as a single April 1979. From the album "Spirits Having Flown," released February 1979.

"What is this? You might say! Is this the life of a pair of underpants or The Memoirs of a Dodgy Doctor? Close! It was in fact our third number one off the SPIRITS album."

Robin Gibb

MASSACHUSETTS
(B., R. & M. Gibb)

Recorded August 1967. Originally released as a single September 1967. From the album "Horizontal," released February 1968.

"We knocked out this little gem on our first promo trip to New York. We had just checked into the St. Regis Hotel, very excited to be in America and having little else to do. Interesting flower power reflections, good times, etc."

Barry Gibb

MELODY FAIR
(B., R. & M. Gibb)

Recorded August 1968. From the album "Odessa," released March 1969.

"From the Motion Picture MELODY, or S.W.A.L.K., David Putnam's first film. He used a lot of our earlier singles. A lovely movie based on kids falling in love for the first time. This is, I think, one of our best productions in simplicity and warmth."

Maurice Gibb

MORE THAN A WOMAN
(B,. R. & M. Gibb)

Recorded Spring 1977. From the album "Saturday Night Fever," released November 1977.

"This is a song we wrote with unimaginable results. Tavares had a big hit with it. One of the songs that made SATURDAY NIGHT FEVER such a success, and when the whole world was dancing."

Maurice Gibb

MR. NATURAL
(B. & R. Gibb)

Recorded January 1974. Originally released as a single February 1974. From the album "Mr. Natural," released July 1974.

"Enter our 'knee-pad' era.
Time: 1974
Situation: Desperate.
Answer: New LP.
Label: Atlantic
Single: Mr. Natural
Situation: Desperate."

Robin Gibb

MY WORLD
(B. & R. Gibb)

Recorded October 1971. Originally released as a single January 1972. From the album "Best Of Bee Gees Vol. 2," released June 1973.

"One rollicking little jaunt that me and the lads came up with in downtown Birmingham, England, whilst doing a television show called GOLDEN SHOT, the ensuing result being that it went on to be a huge top 20 hit in the UK and the US that left the three of us 'drooling' with pleasure."

Robin Gibb

NEW YORK MINING DISASTER 1941
(R. & B. Gibb)

Recorded March 1967. Originally released as a single April 1967. From the album "Bee Gees 1st," released July 1967.

"Written on the back stairway of Polydor Records, March 1967. Robert Stigwood had just signed us to Nems and we were there to do demos for our album (Bee Gees 1st). The song itself was really about the Aberfan mining disaster in Wales, killing over two hundred children. Quite sad really."

Barry Gibb

NIGHT FEVER
(B., R. & M. Gibb)

Recorded Spring 1977. Released as a single February 1978. From the album "Saturday Night Fever," released November 1977.

See "Stayin' Alive"

Barry Gibb

NIGHTS ON BROADWAY
(B., R. & M. Gibb)

Recorded January 1975. Released as a single September 1975. From the album "Main Course," released June 1975.

"This is one of my all time Bee Gees favourites! From the Main Course LP. This song holds a special place for a variety of factors...One, the start of a long, lasting relationship with producer Arif Mardin. The second, that it enabled the Bee Gees to get back to their R&B/Soul roots, which in the previous years we had neglected; and thirdly, I think it was just a well constructed record and song! And if I may say so...one to be proud of."

Robin Gibb

ONE
(B., R. & M. Gibb)

Recorded 1988. From the album "One," released 1989.

"This song brought us back to US radio. A leading media paper recently stated regarding this song, "The Bee Gees are capable of at least one more hit." I don't believe that, I believe we could have at least two."

Barry Gibb

(OUR LOVE) DON'T THROW IT ALL AWAY
(B. Gibb & B. Weaver)

Recorded 1977. From the album "Bee Gees Greatest," released October 1979.

"This was written in France at the FEVER sessions with Blue Weaver. Andy did an excellent version of it."

Barry Gibb

RUN TO ME
(B., R. & M. Gibb)

Recorded April 1972. Originally released as a single, July 1972. From the album "To Whom It May Concern," released October 1972.

"This song was written at a time when most rock acts were trying to play it safe in terms of crafting top 40 records, and in a sense could only have been recorded in 1972.

However, having said that...it still boasts a rather infectious chorus... don't you think?"

Robin Gibb

SOMEONE BELONGING TO SOMEONE
(B., R. & M. Gibb)

Recorded 1983. Released as a single August 1983. From the album "Stayin' Alive," released July 1983.

"Fair ballad from a silly film."

Barry Gibb

STAYIN' ALIVE
(B., R. & M. Gibb)

Recorded Spring 1977. Released as a single December 1977. From the album "Saturday Night Fever," released November 1977.

"Great steaming medallions and disco boots, what do we have here? The most dangerous record of the seventies. Place record on turntable, light fuse and stand well back."

Barry Gibb

THROW A PENNY
(B. & R. Gibb)

Recorded December 1973. Released as a single July 1974. From the album "Mr. Natural," released July 1974.

"Where are we going?"

Barry Gibb

TO LOVE SOMEBODY
(R. & B. Gibb)

Recorded March 1967. Originally released as a single June 1967. From the album "Bee Gees 1st," released July 1967.

"Conceived in New York (1967) for Otis Redding after meeting him with a view to writing a song for him. This is a great example of a song having a life of its own."

Barry Gibb

TOO MUCH HEAVEN
(B., R. & M. Gibb)

Recorded March-November 1978. Originally released as a single November 1978. From the album "Spirits Having Flown," released February 1979.

"The starving children of the world was the genesis of this song. 1979, early in the evolution of music charity efforts, we donated this one to UNICEF and its worldwide work which we felt strongly about. And, it was a huge hit, too!"

Robin Gibb

TRAGEDY
(B., R. & M. Gibb)

Recorded March-November 1978. Released as a single February 1979. From the album "Spirits Having Flown," released February 1979.

"I've always loved singles and to me this represents the 'classic' single...high urgency, one-word-statement chorus line, with an equally contagious verse. I love this record."

Robin Gibb

THE WOMAN IN YOU
(B., R. & M. Gibb)

Recorded 1983. Originally released as a single, May 1983. From the album "Staying Alive," released July 1983.

"One of our contributions to the 'Rocky in Legwarmers' movie; unfortunately the director misused it and our co-producers did the same."

Maurice Gibb

WORLD
(B., R. & M. Gibb)

Recorded October 1967. Originally released as a single November 1967. From the album "Horizontal," released February 1968.

"A song we recorded in '67. Vivid memories of Robin's great performance on the organ, and me playing a very compressed piano (which we also used on WORDS.) A big thank you to Mike Clayton, our engineer, for helping us in the making of this little epic."

Maurice Gibb

WORDS
(B., R. & M. Gibb)

Recorded October 1967. Originally released as a single January 1968. From the album "Best of Bee Gees," released October 1969.

"This came about at the Adams Row, London, home of Robert Stigwood. Robert had the gift of bringing out the very best in any artist, and I feel this particular song justified his faith in us. This song's for you Rob."

Barry Gibb

YOU SHOULD BE DANCING (LONG VERSION)
(B., R. & M. Gibb)

Recorded January 1976. Originally released as a single June 1976. From the album "Children Of The World," released September 1976.

"You can't take songs like this too seriously. It was actually a very exhilarating time, settling in Miami. We had a great band and this song came from that feeling."

Barry Gibb

Discography

THE BEE GEES SING AND PLAY 14 BARRY GIBB SONGS (1965)

BEE GEES 1st (1967)

HORIZONTAL (1968)

IDEA (1968)

RARE, PRECIOUS AND BEAUTIFUL (1968)

ODESSA (1969)

BEST OF THE BEE GEES (1969)

RARE, PRECIOUS AND BEAUTIFUL, VOLUME 2 (1970)

RARE, PRECIOUS AND BEAUTIFUL, VOLUME 3 (1970)

ROBIN'S REIGN (ROBIN GIBB) (1970)

CUCUMBER CASTLE (1970)

2 YEARS ON (1970)

TRAFALGAR (1971)

TO WHOM IT MAY CONCERN (1972)

LIFE IN A TIN CAN (1973)

BEST OF THE BEE GEES, VOLUME 2 (1973)

A KICK IN THE HEAD IS WORTH EIGHT IN THE PANTS (1973, UNRELEASED)

MR. NATURAL (1974)

MAIN COURSE (1975)

CHILDREN OF THE WORLD (1976)

BEE GEES GOLD (1976)

HERE AT LAST...BEE GEES...LIVE (1977)

SATURDAY NIGHT FEVER (1977)

SPIRITS HAVING FLOWN (1979)

BEE GEES GREATEST (1979)

LIVING EYES (1981)

HOW OLD ARE YOU? (ROBIN GIBB) (1983)

STAYING ALIVE (1983)

SECRET AGENT (ROBIN GIBB) (1984)

NOW VOYAGER (BARRY GIBB) (1984)

WALLS HAVE EYES (ROBIN GIBB) (1985)

E-S-P (1987)

HAWKS (BARRY GIBB) (1988)

ONE (1989)